Also by David W. Berner

Fiction

The Islander
Rainbow Man
Night Radio
Sandman
A Well-Respected Man
Things Behind the Sun

Nonfiction/Memoir

Daylight Saving Time
Accidental Lessons
Any Road Will Take You There
There's a Hamster in the Dashboard
October Song
The Consequence of Stars
Walks With Sam

Garden Tools

poems by

David W. Berner

Finishing Line Press
Georgetown, Kentucky

Garden Tools

Copyright © 2025 by David W. Berner
ISBN 979-8-89990-131-7 First Edition

All rights reserved under International and Pan-American Copyright Conventions. No part of this book may be reproduced in any manner whatsoever without written permission from the publisher, except in the case of brief quotations embodied in critical articles and reviews.

ACKNOWLEDGMENTS

I am thankful for all the poets I have read, for they have shown me the power of verse. I especially want to thank the poet John Muro for his keen eye and his gentle nudges through the many drafts of these poems. His brilliance helped me find my voice. And always, I am grateful to Leslie, my wife, whose spirit runs through every stanza in this volume.

Thanks to the following journals and anthologies where these poems were first published.

Symphony of Seasons, Wingless Dreamer: "Desert Prayer," "In the Garden," and "The Last Tulip."
Humans of the World: "At the Window."
Letting Go and Moving On, Poet's Choice: "For the Writer," and "Neighbor."
Red Noise Collective: "Scarlett Johansson."
Cathexis Northwest Press: "Gift of a Day."

Publisher: Leah Huete de Maines
Editor: Christen Kincaid
Cover Art: Canva.com/Artist: @vasile-saptefrati
Author Photo: David W. Berner
Cover Design: Elizabeth Maines McCleavy

Order online: www.finishinglinepress.com
also available on amazon.com

Author inquiries and mail orders:
Finishing Line Press
PO Box 1626
Georgetown, Kentucky 40324
USA

Poems

Landscape

Desert Prayer 1
The Last Tulip 2
Before the Rain 3
Clouds 4
Dog Dreams 5
Early Enough 6
In the Garden 7
Workshop 8
Illness 9
Fists 10
The Last of Winter 11
The Innocence 12
Neighbor 13
At the Window 14
For the Writer 15
Garden Tools 16
Sunday Omelet 17
Gift of a Day 18

Love

Half Moon 21
If a Father Cries 23
If I Had a Walking Stick 24
If I Had the Morning 25
March Morning 26

Old Man, Sick Dog 27

Pink Morning 28

Reading Thomas Merton in the Backyard Shed 29

Scarlett Johansson 30

Sunglasses in the Woods 31

The Dream 32

Thinking of My Death 33

Waiting 34

Once a Boat 35

Mother's Day 36

One Apple 37

Memorial Day 38

Chicagohenge 39

Bicycle in the Rain 40

Last Day of School 41

Longing

Stopping for Lemonade 45

Driving to the City at 3 a.m. 46

Magnolia Blossoms 47

Baseball on the Radio 48

On the Morning When the Tornado Warning Siren is Tested ... 49

A Friend Arrives 50

Portrait of My Father on His Wedding Day 51

When the Reverend Walks Near Dylan's Grave 52

Gone Walking 53

Ashes from a Fire 54

December 55

Annihilating all that's made / To a green thought in a green shade

—Andrew Marvell

Landscape

Desert Prayer

If I were to swallow the earth,
I would taste cinnamon in the
desert's red rocks,
where the light catches
the edges of the heart,
and the table is set for one.

If I were to swallow the earth,
I would drink from the river
in the hollowed canyon,
where minerals gather
to nourish the spirits,
and save them from the world so mad.

If I were to swallow the earth,
I would savor the sweet spine
of the sagebrush,
where the mule deer
comes to feed,
and searches the spring for the aster.

If I were to swallow the earth,
I would stand on the mountain,
above the arroyo,
where rainbows touch land to sky,
and breathe in the holy ghosts of the dead.

First published in the 2024 poetry anthology, "Symphony of Seasons"

The Last Tulip

From the deep-brown ground comes
an owl-brown, dying plant, dying for now,
and after a long sleep and the newest spring,
oranges and yellows arise.

But for now, the dying is on, feeding future
births, and in the temporary death,
stands the last, one un-blossomed ovary,
petal-less still, taking its time to awaken
late in its life or fall to the earth.

On the first day of June, it refuses to obey
the rules, the consequences of which will
gift a longer life than the others,
but there is an uncertain death—
a burning in the night or a slow goodbye
without ever opening in the midday sun.

Before the Rain

It's going to rain again,
just look at the bruised sky
and the shadows of gray lurking above the trees.
When it comes it will gather
with what last night's storms left in the street,
in the saturated mulch,
where the primrose are trying to show themselves,
alongside the dead elm tree roots
that no longer nurture its veiny wood.
I wonder where the children are,
the ones who played in the puddles of my boyhood,
the ones who peddled through sidewalk streams,
and I wonder if they know it is going to rain.

Clouds

Clouds hang like smoke from fires
of damp leaves and rain-soaked bark,
holding close a moody joy.

And beyond the haze the sun awaits
for its moment to pounce and save me,
but I wish not to be saved.

There is little that gives one more grace
than acceptance and the embrace of
the blanket, comforting one from false gods.

Dog Dreams

Two squirrels scamper along the fence,
the dog, alerted, stiffens her back and neck.
Instinct has her considering the chase of an ancient wolf,
but her hopes are only dreams,
and her desires only foolish.
She believes in herself, but I know better,
and the squirrels know, too, laughing their way
back to the tree.

And in the relentless glare of a low sun,
promises are lost in the distant fire,
burning the edges of imaginings.
holding yearnings just beyond a desperate reach.

Early Enough

It's early enough
for the robins to have much to say.
It's early enough
for the frost-painted ground to crackle under bare feet.

It's early enough
for the sun to be a divine fire it can never be again.
And it is early enough to think of how
it's never early enough when you're old.

I accept the daylight and
revere the desperate chill that keeps the senses from dulling.
And pray to the knock of a dedicated woodpecker
pounding his way to his own death.

In the Garden

to Leslie

In the garden I hold your hand,
waiting for your heart to float away,
watching your eyes look elsewhere,
knowing I have lost what held me together.

Why are you here, they ask,
on this forever wedding day.
Because I've always been, I say,
because I have always been letting go.

It has never been the end,
this decomposition of the garden,
russet petals falling to the dirt,
the slow decay of a tender heart.

First published in the 2024 poetry anthology "Symphony of Seasons."

Workshop

> *for Father*

Nails rusted together in an old jam jar,
nuts and bolts of every kind in a cigar box,
all of them gathered like Cheerios.

Three hammers of different sizes,
one on the wooden bench,
two on big hooks
on the wall.

A jig saw,
coping saw,
keyhole saw,
and a bone saw.

All these together
in the tiny windowless room
where hands once shaped wood
and a mind ran free.

He decided long ago
he was to be a woodworker,
a carpenter who made
dining room tables, rocking horses, and humidors.

When he died, my mother shut the door,
lost the key,
and tried to forget
what had been left to dust and darkness.

And many years from now
when the house falls in upon itself
and the strangers come
to claim the treasures,

No one will be left to remember
what his hands once built
behind the door
when no one was looking.

Illness

Body wracked
Bed for hours
Fever ridden
Lost a day

Awakened
To a cleanse
Renewal of spirit
Sudden aliveness

Embrace the illness
Until it releases
And showers the body
With holy waters of repair

What tells us
When it's time
To restart a life
To shed a skin?

Revival comes
In the desperate places
Found in the underbelly
Of sickness.

Fists

for Joey

We stood on opposite sides
of the elementary school yard
our hands clenched and outstretched

Running straight to each other
as fast as we could
embracing with the smashing fists

It was our first time
finding pleasure in pain
giggling until we cried

Friends forever, it seemed
until we grew up
and he inhaled the smoke of opium

And I drove away to college
and he lost a brother to heroin
and another in a car accident

I wonder now if he remembers
the fists in the playground
and how we laughed.

And I wonder now if I understood
what I was losing back then
in the dark shadows of cruel innocence.

The Last of Winter

In dimmest light
The crow caws
Angry that it snowed overnight

The crow had other ideas, you see,
It had smelled spring
A particular magic crow trick

But God had other plans
To deaden the scent of the budding, fertile ground
Birders say a crow holds a grudge

It knows when it has been wronged
God needs to be more careful about when
he allows it to snow.

The Innocence

for Saige

You lie on the grass
with eyes closed
and your hair upon my lap,
in radiant innocence.

You smile to the indifferent world
with no troubles to know
as the sun touches your face
in the warmth of innocence.

When you grow taller than the roses
and life first breaks your heart,
hold on to the innocence
and wrap your arms around the clouds.

Blow them away, and pray
to the gods who nurture it
and carry it with you always
until you can no longer carry it alone.

Then give it away to the new little ones
as they might pass it along
to all the broken souls
with innocence blooming.

Neighbor

The home next door has a new owner
And there is a car in the driveway,
And an old man tinkers in the garage
Sometimes he's in the backyard clearing
Fallen branches, that's when my dog barks
She's not used to someone being there
It's been a silent house for months now
The previous owner died, a stroke, they say
He was alive when they carried him out on a stretcher
But his health could not hold.
So now, new hands have come
To bring again this house to life
Since the dead are unable to do so.

At the Window

At the window
as pellets from the frozen rain
assault the glass

Across the hill
I see the man in a hooded coat
surely wishing he had a quicker gait

Along the path
with the icy wind behind
praying he will discover

What he'd lost
somewhere at the start
when his heart had been broken

When all seemed true
and yet it never was
and he aches with recognition

From where he walks
he sees me, too,
across the lawn toward the window

And every time
when the rain comes
both of us search for tiny pieces

Of something akin to wonder
so the storm can't hold us down
or toss us to icy earth

At the window
watching the man in the rain
longing for new chances.

For the Writer

Upon my mat
before a candle
incense drawn from flame
a woodpecker working
in the half-night of pine
its rattle and crack

And on my desk
a typewriter sits
my journal at its side
pen before the page
in the mystic
I dream of magic

For if I saint
or devil's best
I forever hammer
at the bark
in silent night
or morning moon

My beak against the wood.

Garden Tools

At the kitchen sink
I clean the garden tools,
dirt from last season
on a trowel,
clumps of summer grass
on shears.

Yesterday's flowers
are in the shadows,
memories of what once
lived in earth,
remembrances of flashes
of color.

My wife will plant
again this spring,
as she always does,
and these tools will
return to their proper purpose,
and deliver new seeds of promise.

And new blooms of hope
yet, I will always celebrate past bouquets,
flowers of another time,
lingering in my daydreams,
the markers of seasons
and the great return.

Sunday Omelet

Three eggs
a drop of oak milk
a dab of water
whipped in a bowl

Lots of spinach
lots of feta
a tiny bit runny
it is her wish

Virgin olive oil
old steel pan
a slow, low heat
a delicate flip

It is the dish of ancient Persia
France
India
China
Italy
with origins from 1300 AD

Still, today there is only one omelet
awakening senses of a woman
her mouth
her lips
the shine of her cheek
the colors of her hair
the tilt of her smile
that could only be more sublime
if we were in Spain.

Gift of a Day

It is on a walk
that I encounter her
"What a gift of a day," she says

Her smile is true
her stride is deliberate
allowing for wonder

"It is," I say and return a smile.

Winter had forgotten herself,
confused, she was.
Certainly, it cannot always be this way
glorious sun in a season of shadows.

On the walk home I discover a field mouse,
gray and stiff, upon the concrete sidewalk
With tenderness, I slide the body to the nearby
grass and dirt, a more fitting burial, it seems.

Everything ends,
Everything changes, they say

Steps from my door, I wonder
if the mouse had known what a gift
the day had been.

First published in Cathexis Northwest Press

Love

Half Moon

Out my kitchen window
there's a half moon
hanging from the pre-dawn sky.

Up early, again, I am.

It's been that way for days,
pulling away sheets,
rising before the light.

At first, I wondered
why I could no longer sleep,
but now, before the window, I know.

Mother used to say that
the Man in the Moon
was watching us.

If true, today he sees me
with only his one good eye,
and a crooked half-smile.

Tomorrow he'll be there, again,
winking, examining me, even as he wears
his orbital motion as an eye patch.

He must be thinking—why does this old man
wake to the world when so many
are still cocooning in beds?

It's an easy answer when the birdsong is sweet,
the air is cool, and the tulips are opening again for another day,
easy because there is no other time.

When the heart is at its fullest,
or passion so divine,
and before everything changes,

I'm waving to you, Mr. Half Moon,
from here at the window,
with my soul so open to promise.

If a Father Cries

It's not because he remembers his children's tears,
or because he has been forgotten or dismissed,
he cries because of happy memories—the twinkle
in his son's eyes on Christmas day,
the wonder of the tooth fairy's silver dollar gift.

If a father cries, it's because he sees what
fathers before him have endured or neglected,
or how a man becomes the father before him without
effort, without noticing, until it is either too late,
too obvious, or too devastating.

If a father cries, it's because he can no longer hear
his own father's whispers from the grave,
carrying the wisdom of age or catastrophic love
that has eroded the statues of gods,
and crippled the angel in flight.

If a father cries, it's because he has come to know
that there is no release from his heavenly heights,
his perch far above his children's lives,
where he watches with a hand-turned wooden bowl
to catch the falling ashes.

If I Had a Walking Stick

My grandmother carried a shillelagh,
a cudgel of oak, a cane to lean upon.
And when she died, my father asked if
I would care to have her walking stick.

The canes of Dickens and of Wilde,
the crutch of Chaplin and of Churchill,
canes of adornment, of balance, the jewelry
of the artist, the thinker, and the dreamer.

In a basement closet the shillelagh rests,
holding memories of forgotten walks.
No journeys have yet been made with it
at my side, but one day that will change.

On sturdy hardwood I will rest my weight,
and grip it with my trembling hands
to transform the past to present day,
and believe in the power of ancient, shared burdens.

If I Had the Morning

I would stand upon the edge of the sea,
and face the wind, and watch the gulls
dance in the silver sky, and I would breathe
the salt and taste the mist, and declare
that I am timeless.

And as the day grows longer and the sun
has climbed high enough, I would fall asleep
along the cliffs, and listen to the sweep
of gulls who sail above my aging
heart that longs for another
day like this.

Howth, Ireland
Summer, 2023

March Morning

I walk across the frosted grass
It stings of early March
The morning is young
And I am old.

Why am I naked below the ankles
on a still-winter Midwest morning?

I thought about this
before I headed out today
and the answer is a simple one.

The icy bite reminds me
that I am alive
and tomorrow morning
the frost will be gone.

Old Man, Sick Dog

It is the middle of the night and
the dog crawls in bed with me,
nestling her nose to my side,
her paw stretching out to touch my chest.

I pet her head, scratch her neck,
and tell her it is okay.

One never really knows if things are okay,
only telling ourselves it must be, it must be.

In time, she is asleep and so am I,
and in the morning, both of our hearts
are still beating.

Pink Morning

I had always been indifferent about the color,
the hue of a baby's blanket,
the too delicate rose,
the lipstick of questionable women.
But on a walk minutes before sunrise,
the cirrus clouds low on the northern horizon
are suffused with the day's first light,
and I think differently now
about this unexpected
shade of the akoya pearl,
hanging on the treetops
in the quiet when no one is awake
to question my change of heart.

Reading Thomas Merton in the Backyard Shed

The chill of morning surrounds me,
the incense burns a silver blue.
It is Thomas who has allowed me
to contemplate,
to find the God in me.

But I am still unsure that God is here,
if he presents himself at the altar
or as a butterfly in the rain.

So, I seek the holy unknown
and search for signs of light,
and possess the words of Merton,
Thoreau, and Thich Nhat Hanh
and wait for whispers.

Scarlett Johansson

I dreamt that Scarlett Johansson was my friend
She worked in a tavern and gave Easter eggs to children
I admired her

I hoped for her to see the good in me
But she was tentative about how close we should be
She thought differently of me, she said, after I told her
how my great, great, great Irish grandfather had married a young girl

Very young

It was not unusual after the potato famine, I told her
How can you judge me on decisions made so long ago
when the cultural norms were so misguided?

Still, in the dream, she walked away from me, carrying roses in her hand,
a gift from an admirer

I should have given her roses.

First published in The Red Noise Collective

Sunglasses in the Woods

Someone lost their sunglasses in the woods
Another hiker hung them on a trail sign
"Here they are," they must have said as they placed
them where other hikers might see.

Tortoise shell frames
Lenses dark and brown
They don't appear expensive
but are nicely made, it seems.

Man's? Woman's?
Does it matter?
Are they yours?

I wonder how long they'll remain on the trail sign.
Will a park ranger take them to the lost and found?

Or will they stay here for days, for weeks,
until the snow melts and blossoms emerge,
and the hiker returns with no memory of what had been lost,
giving up long ago after searching coat pockets,
and the glove compartment, and the backpack.

"There they are!" the hiker will say in discovery,
placing them on his nose to see the once unseen,
and the woods as he never has before.

Morton Arboretum, Glen Ellyn, Illinois

The Dream

I waved my hand and there were flowers,
blue and gold and deep maroon.
And every time I gestured, more flowers
bloomed anew.

Each time my heart burst open,
joy tumbled out to nourish the roots.
And as I fully awoke,
my elated heart held to the
exaltation like the moon holds
to the sky, like the child holds
the mother's hand.

For hours my soul was replete,
spilling promise into air.

But by late morning, all that had
made me deliriously drunk had been
burned away by the rising sun and come noon
I had found that dreams can only be
realized when you are prepared
for magic.

Thinking of My Death

My sister's ashes are in a plastic box
on the backseat floor of my car.
I ride around with her there to the gas station,
the grocery store for bananas,
the dentist to have my teeth cleaned.
They'd been under the nightstand for years,
but it got weird thinking she was there
in my bedroom where my wife and I sleep.
The ashes are waiting for when
I find the right places to spread them—
the mountain slope where she skied,
the woodland trail where she walked,
the stream where she fished.

Until then they'll travel with me around the block,
and my sister will hear the music on the radio,
my conversations with my wife about
the weather and the neighbors,
and if God exists.

I hope someone drives me around when I'm dead.

Waiting

I let the dog out
again

Third time this morning
and again, she stands
at the storm door glass
waiting

I had a dog years ago
that cried at the door
and another that scratched
until I came to the rescue

But this dog only
waits

When I'm in line at the grocery store
or the bank
or the drive-thru coffee shop
or the doctor's office waiting room
I'll think of her eyes,
dark and full of longing,
and her steady stare,
and her stance so still.

Once a Boat

I dreamt of floating across the lake,
of leaping off the bow into green-blue water
bare-chested in the sun
and as the wind glided me along the waves,
I wore one of those captain's caps
the white kind with the black rim
and sported boat shoes like jaunty New Englanders wear,

But the truth is, I couldn't catch a breeze
and my sail fell limp in the middle of the lake,
the sailboat could only drift in the meager current
with no gasoline in the small engine's tank,
there I was with nothing left to do
but tug on a line and swim to shore.

That summer I sold my dream
to another dreamer.

Mother's Day

He brought his folding chair to the graveyard,
whispering to his dead mother at her headstone,
buried there years before when he was young.

If she can hear him, be it in heaven or hell,
she has certainly forgiven him for what had been,
for what is now, or what will never be.

All that time wasted, and tears unspoken,
and the love that was there despite it all,
rising through the fallow ground.

As the sun falls and prayers have been said,
he will gather his chair and carry it away until
another Mother's Day or until his own heart rests.

One Apple

She fed the dog
tiny apple slices
meant for her

Every time I gave her one
she stretched out her tiny hand
toward the dog's open mouth

Thank you for the treat, the dog must have been thinking.

Who is this little girl who can hardly stand,
who walks with a waddle, who talks in mumbles,
and smiles with every step?

She must know what
kindness is
She must know how
to be generous
She must know the secret
to happiness

She knows exactly how to live,
this little girl,
one apple at a time.

Memorial Day

My cousin was an Air Force mechanic who worked on fighter planes,
stationed in Saigon during the war.
He was frightened to go to sleep, distressed by the dead bodies
in military caskets on the tarmac waiting to be flown home.

When my cousin returned from his tour,
the family threw a party on his parents' front lawn.
We all drank beer in the sun, slapped him
on the back, and thanked God that he was safe.

Years later in a movie theater,
we watched Oliver Stone's film on the war.
Viewing the vacant eyes of soldiers emerging from the jungle,
my cousin whispered, "I can still smell the bodies."

Chicagohenge

The sun nestles in the cracks
of concrete monsters reaching for clouds,
in the city that birthed the skyscraper,
where beefy men owned all the taverns.

Rough and murderous is its past,
its present riddled with street bullets.
Yet on a clear spring day
the light of the closest star winks off glass,
and there is beauty in what remains.

Bicycle in the Rain

Classes long been dismissed,
school doors securely locked,
and against the playground fence,
rests a bike, its body glimmering
in the rain.

Many days will pass, and summer will come,
and on an early Sunday morning in July,
a child will recall his forgotten ride,
and run to find it untouched but tangled
in the overgrowth.

And on the way back home,
the sun will warm steel handlebars,
offer fuel to stiffened pedals,
and the child will smile, reunited
with a breeze.

Last Day of School

Two girls ride bikes,
'round and 'round the streets,
up and down and over,
laughing, calling each other's names.

They zip by with their feet off the pedals,
flirting with minor dangers,
snaking their way along the hard pavement,
slowing only slightly at the crossroads.

School has not yet rung the morning bell,
for the half-day of goodbyes before the break,
but the girls are already celebrating,
already rejoicing summer.

I think now of my last days of school,
and the friends who left for good, moving to other towns,
never to return to Mr. Madison's classroom.

Longing

Stopping for Lemonade

Making a wrong turn,
onto a street with no sidewalks,
I see two girls excitedly
waving their hands,
one opening a colorful umbrella.

I drive closer and there
at the end of a driveway,
is a small table and
taped to its edge is a handmade sign:
Lemonade for Sale.

How much? I ask.
A dollar, a smiling girl says.
I hand the other the only bill
in my wallet and reach for a plastic cup
of yellow liquid and a straw.

When I was a boy many years ago,
I sold lemonade for twenty-five cents,
and for hours no one came.
Then a truckload of construction workers
arrived and bought all I had.

Driving to the City at 3 a.m.

On the expressway that crosses into the city from the west,
someone has set off fireworks along the side of the highway.
They blast into the night—sparkles and shimmering torches.
Out of the darkness and into the shattering, walks a shirtless man,
stumbling along the white lines of the freeway, unaware of the flashing
headlights and the drivers who have never seen such a thing,
the fantastic light show and the bare-chested man determined
to march against speeding traffic under a crackling sky
on a hot summer night in Chicago.

Magnolia Blossoms

For a week they shine among the green leaves,
but soon they fall, soft like white Dandelion seeds,
floating and gathering to form pink pillows
on the ground, under the branches, in the sun,
until they decay to a wounded brown and blow away
in the breeze of a dying spring and forgotten in
a summer of waiting and waiting until the autumn shakes
the leaves away and winter buries our memories.

Baseball on the Radio

A black and silver transistor,
the antenna stretched to the sky,
rested on our house's front stoop,
and from its speakers came the call,
a rope into the outfield, a stand-up double,
and Roberto Clemente had his 3000th hit,
the final hit before he would die
in a plane crash three months
later while on his way to help earthquake
victims in Nicaragua.

I still have the old transistor radio,
its antenna broken, its speaker
hisses with age, the tuner cannot always
find a signal, but when it does,
and I discover on a late summer afternoon,
a voice filled with glory from a distant diamond,
I think about my days on the stoop,
holding tight to a young boy's wonder.

On a Morning When the Tornado Warning Siren is Tested

With coffee, I sit,
still, meditative
until the sky sings,
a chant from the treetops,
a dangerous *om*,
prolonged and wavering.

For minutes it wails,
like monks in prayer,
asking the gods for forgiveness,
for shelter from our storms,
for the children to hide in bathtubs,
for grandmothers to cower in basements.

To live in the path
of the twisting clouds
requires a warning each month,
a test to be certain that
when the world spins out of control
we are ready.

I wonder now as the sun arrives
from behind mad morning clouds,
what warnings I have failed to hear,
what sirens have howled, disregarded,
despite their ghastly screams.

A Friend Arrives

On my shirt collar it lands,
this bug of flight,
its translucent wings,
and its fire-red grotesque eyes.

For a moment I watch,
and it watches back,
as its wings flutter,
proving its place.

It is in a pause,
no fear and purpose,
two beings in the morning sun,
aware of each other's beating hearts.

But just as quickly,
I react as most might do,
and flip the bug away
with the flick of a finger and thumb.

It lands on the grass,
startled by dismissal,
and I am immediately stricken
with gloom and regret.

Saddened that I would reject
what came to me in surprise,
new in the day what
might have been in my yesterday.

Portrait of My Father on His Wedding Day

It is in his eyes, something, a smile, yet not,
standing stiff in a white jacket.
thin as a reed, delicate, shy, yet not,
falling lace from her delicate hair.

Wide-brimmed hat upon her mother's head,
her father, sturdy in his posture, certain,
his mother in a flowered dress, tiny bonnet,
holding tight to her white clutch.

What is in his eyes, my father?
What can he not see, or see so well?
His missing father is a ghost,
retreating, forgotten, for now.

When just a boy, he walked away,
his father lighting cigarettes for another,
dancing to different love songs,
missing from a wedding day.

When the Reverend Walks Near Dylan's Grave

Alone with the moss-covered graves of St. Martin's
I search for the white cross on a hill.
From the ancient trees, like a grounded great bird,
the holy man strides tall in the shadows,
his graying hair, long and ponytailed,
holding a Bible, he smiles a blessed smile.

Searching for the resting place of the poet,
he must assume, or a loved one
with an ancestral link, over the walkway
and through the black iron gate,
across the slope above the freshly dead,
among the stones atop the sleepy town,
just over the hill from the writing shed,
and its ghostly verses,
stands the milky crucifix alone,
seashell jewels adorning the dirt.

It is then that the pale sky
touches me with tears,
tiny drops of sacred translucent blood
from a million messengers crying.

Laugharne, Wales

Gone Walking

Around the corner near the train track,
   along the gravel where the road crew repaves the street,
     near the pond where the blue heron lurks and fishes,
       around the church where someone
         has placed a wreath for the dead.

It's a walk
not an epiphany
not a solitary gift
not meditation
but a walk
pure
unadorned
take the dog
revolt against purpose
stop pretending.

Ashes from a Fire

I am six years old
bare feet touch the cold
hardwood floor
pans rattle in the kitchen below
breakfast, Mum calls.

I am twelve years old
alone on the porch
watching black-and-white
baseball at Forbes Field
rounding third, heading home.

I am eighteen years old
in love, I am
fog of desperation
if only for a smile
if only for a kiss.

I am thirty-three years old
my son's hand in mine
his eyes filled with awe
as fireworks burst
on the night of the Fourth.

I am forty-five years old
alone and sorry
not for me, but for them
in their beds in the dark
wondering how it will be.

I am sixty years old
in love again, I am
counting heartbeats
in the days that remain
each one for everyone but me.

I am sixty-seven years old
from my bed I see the awakening
a ghost shimmering at the window
snow has fallen overnight
like cinders from a fire.

December

coming on winter
the leaves departed
the wind gray
the garden brown
snow waiting
in the lattice work of clouds
to fall on skeleton reeds
of decayed thistles
stillness takes hold
be silent
pause

David W. Berner is the author of several books of memoir and fiction. He has been the recipient of honors from the Paris Book Festival, the NYC Big Book Award, the Society of Midland Authors, the Chicago Writers Association, the National Association of Independent Writers and Editors, and others. He has been the Writer-in-Residence at the Jack Kerouac Project in Orlando, FL and the Ernest Hemingway Birthplace Home and Museum in Oak Park, IL.

Garden Tools is his first book of poetry.

www.ingramcontent.com/pod-product-compliance
Lightning Source LLC
Chambersburg PA
CBHW030058170426
43197CB00010B/1581